HOME SERIES

HOME SERIES
DESIGNER HOUSES

BETA-PLUS

CONTENTS

P. 4-5
A view of sculptor Mariette Teugels' studio. She works with bronze, polyester, plaster and terracotta to create expressive portraits of joyful people, nudes and ballerinas.

P. 6
A work by Robert Mangold above a table in this house designed by architect Pascal Van der Kelen.

FOREWORD

Designer homes... This book is not just about interior designers, but also about designers and artists from a wide variety of other domains where good design is essential.

Here, the word "designer" is synonymous with creative projects that are distinctive, inspirational and original. The reports in this book feature many different styles, including classic, ultra-contemporary, bohemian and rustic.

These are homes designed with a strong aesthetic and a perfect eye for detail. They represent an extension of the owners' personality and are a powerful form of expression. These thirteen reports feature a number of exceptional designer homes.

P. 8
A rattan daybed by designer Poul Kjaerholm and sculptor Anish Kapoor's Gourds on the wall. A project by Pascal Van der Kelen.

P. 10-11
The private apartment of designer Romeo Sozzi (Promemoria) in Milan.

SPACE AND SUBTLE LUXURY

IN A SCULPTURAL VILLA

C ustom-built interiors are Obumex's field of absolute expertise. This house, designed by the Brussels architect Fabien Van Tomme, is an example of the company's approach. The garden and surroundings are by Buro Groen. Xavier Gadeyne, senior interior architect at Obumex, designed and supervised all of the interior work.

Sumptuous materials, subtle colours and impressive spaces make this home and office a place of luxury and relaxation.

This house forms a timeless and contemporary whole, complemented by modern art from the owner's collection.

The villa was designed by architect Fabien Van Tomme. All of the exterior walls have been plastered. The design features windows with stainless-steel frames and large wooden terraces.
A long wall runs alongside the swimming pool, allowing swimmers a glimpse of the garden and clearly separating the terrace and swimming pool from the garden to create an outdoor room.

Serene, white walls and a bleached, aged oak parquet floor throughout. Art by Albert Mastenbroek (left) and Jörg Döring (above).

P. 18-19
Reading corner with chaises longues by
Christian Liaigre.
Fitted floor-to-ceiling cupboards.

The office with a custom-built suspended cupboard unit in a glossy white finish and a desk in dark-stained oak, made for this project by Obumex. This room is an essential element of the living area, but sliding panels can be used to close it off.

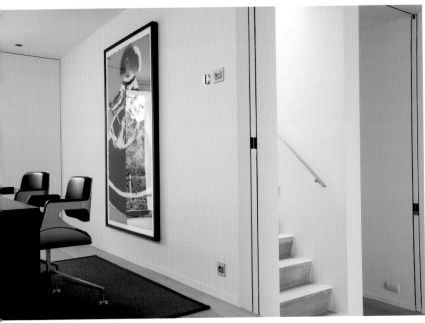

Sitting area with black Promemoria sofas and white leather armchairs by Christian Liaigre on a cotton carpet. Gas fire with a low view through to the swimming pool.

The dining table was designed and created by Obumex, combined with black-tinted Y chairs by Hans J. Wegner.

A view from the parents' bedroom into the garden and the downstairs sitting area.

This pivoting mirrored door at the end of the upstairs corridor creates an impression of space.

The parents' bathroom with two "Wash" washstands, designed by Vincent Van Duysen for Obumex.

The shower is finished in white Carrara marble.

THE ART OF AUTHENTICITY

IN A 1742 TOWNHOUSE

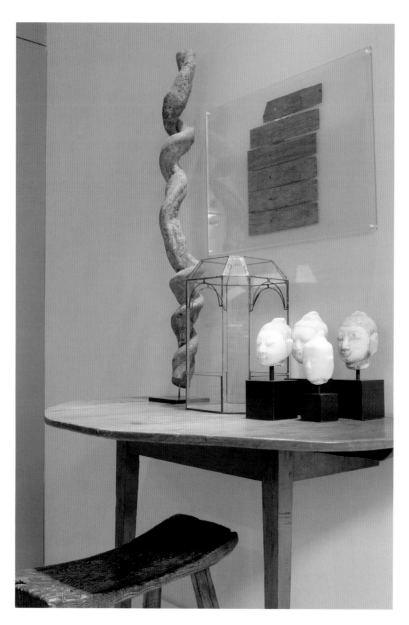

A lex Van De Walle is a structural engineer by training. He specialises in the renovation of distinctive houses and has a particular preference for old-fashioned, traditional constructions and timeworn, sensual materials.

His own living and working space is a beautiful showcase for his skills and perfectly illustrates his constant quest for authenticity and unaffected beauty. This property dates back to 1742, but seems even older, as many of its elements reveal a medieval influence.

The whole house has a remarkable atmosphere: streamlined and almost casual; unaffected, yet opulent.

The house is in shades of grey. Above the fireplace, a nineteenth-century work and two ceramic statues from China. Right, a garden ornament in concrete.

P. 28-29
Alex Van De Walle has a preference for timeworn, distinctive objects that are placed in a new context. Art is very important in his designs, because of the elegance and atmosphere that it adds to an interior.

Left of the desk, a work by Axel Dumont.

Alex Van De Walle has combined these different objects to create a surprising, yet harmonious display.

P. 30
The house dates from the eighteenth century, but the archaic construction style makes it appear far older. Alex Van De Walle has created an atmospheric workspace on the ground floor. Left, an eighteenth-century Chinese family portrait, with red Zulu hats beside it and on the shelves. In the foreground, three phalluses on a pedestal. The lighting is by Modular.

The mansard roof is the only element dating from the Enlightenment. The white "canvas" is part of the original roof.

P. 32
A strong instinct for streamlined aesthetics in combination with timeworn objects: an English chair, an old mirror (between the windows) and Chinese mirrors from the twelfth and thirteenth centuries.

Above the gas stove, *La Vache* by Jean-Marc Louis. Next to it, a Chinese mortuary statuette from the Tang period.

Left, two voodoo fetishes from Côte d'Ivoire. Beside them, reclaimed architectural elements from elsewhere in the house.

FROM SPONTANEITY TO HARMONY

J ean-Marc Louis (b. 1959) lived in the African coastal city of Abidjan (Côte d'Ivoire) for twenty-five years before settling in Brussels as an artist.

His long stay in Africa had a major influence on the development of Louis' oeuvre. He still shows a clear preference for earthy shades and rough materials.

Jean-Marc Louis has developed an unusual style based on out-of-the-ordinary materials, such as components of vacuum cleaners or cigarette ends, which form the "ingredients" of monochrome works in which every element finds its own place.

Although Louis likes to work on paper, he does not neglect the canvas. Here, his approach is much broader and full of intense gestures. His frequent use of the "dripping" technique has led him to be viewed as a worthy successor to the abstract expressionists. His colour palette usually remains dark and sober, with a prevalence of shades of brown and grey. This report illustrates the artist's living and working spaces on the basis of three key areas: his studio, the classic nineteenth-century house that he has completely restored, and one of the house's outbuildings.

Jean-Marc Louis uses a brush to sketch characters that suggest the traditional techniques used in eastern calligraphy.

P. 34
Above the oriental console, a work by
Jean-Marc Louis from the series
Paysages. On the right, two bronze
sculptures.

Louis restored the "classic" section of the 19th-century building with great respect, removing false ceilings to reveal all of the original elements.

The courtyard is the route between the classic house on the left and the outbuilding on the right, which Jean-Marc Louis has designed as a hypermodern loft (see photographs on page 37).

A MINIMALIST DESIGNER LOFT

T he projects of interior architect Filip Deslee could be defined as essentialist: a minimalism that extends further than just the design.

This loft, situated in an old ice-cream factory, is a perfect example of his work. The key words here are mass, volume, light, structure and repetition. This aesthetic purism is taken to an extreme, but always remains functional.

Filip Deslee designed the complete interior, including the furniture.

Deslee had the walls painted white and the oak floor treated to create a beautiful, sober result.
Furniture by Le Corbusier and a lounge sofa by Filip Deslee.

The table in the foreground is in aged oak. The surface and the wall above the stove are in rough slate. Work surface in Corian. Vola taps and Lem chairs from La Palma.

Grey-tinted glass separates the office from the bedroom and the shower from the dressing room.

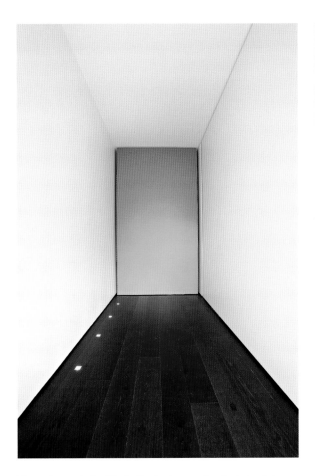

The entrance hall with, in the background, a fuchsia-pink pivoting door that leads to the toilets.

The bathroom floor is in slate.

Filip Deslee designed the bathroom furniture.

THE RESTORATION

OF AN EIGHTEENTH-CENTURY
GENTILHOMMIÈRE

R enowned couturier Edouard Vermeulen (Natan) has lived on the Rozenhout estate for over a decade: an 18th-century gentil-hommière situated in a beautiful park. In close collaboration with architect Raymond Rombouts, the original house was improved and a pavilion was added.

Edouard Vermeulen – himself an interior architect before he made his name in the world of haute couture – created the interior design: a timeless and subdued colour palette, in line with his exclusive collections.

The entrance hall. The floor in this room and the adjoining space is original.

The floor with its chessboard design was found by Stéphane de Harlez (Château de Deulin). The painting came from the shop of Antwerp antiques dealer Frank Van Laer. The chair on the extreme right is from Axel Vervoordt.

P. 46-47
The panelling is also from Stéphane de Harlez, cut to size for this room by architect Rombouts.

Antiques dealers Brigitte and Alain Garnier selected the seats and the cupboard.

P. 48
The floor in this dining room is by
Origines from Paris. Panelling by
Michel Ceuterick. Chairs by Jean-
Philippe De Meyer.

The bathroom is panelled throughout in wood, based on an original idea by Raymond Rombouts.

Polyèdre created the bathroom unit. The original 18th-century wooden floor is from Groep Moris.

The atmosphere is almost monastic in its simplicity.

A cosy guestroom, painted in lime paints by Dankers Decor. The cabinet is by Torus.

THE COUNTRY HOME

OF A FASHION PROFESSIONAL

T his country house was built in the 1920s and belongs to a big name in the world of fashion.

The restoration work took almost a year and was carried out according to the owners' instructions. Esther Gutmer did the interior design for the project.

The decoration reveals modern Art-Deco influences in a palette of white, grey and black.

The walls of the sitting room have a satin plaster finish, creating a mellow atmosphere. The coffee table is a design by Ado Châle.

The fireplace has been finished with black steel on both sides to enhance the hearth effect. The original parquet floor has been retained, but has been polished and coloured in a mahogany shade.

A view of the office. The walls are finished in grey flannel. Furniture in durable wood, polished to a shine.

In the foreground, a Ralph Lauren chair in Kevlar and leather. Art-Deco desk and light.

The ceiling moulding is decorated with gold leaf.
The wall panels conceal storage space. The gold leaf is a fine contrast with the black lacquered wood.

Storage space and a refrigerator are concealed behind the panels of the bar area, which are in navy blue suede. An alcove in black-tinted glass, lit by LED lighting.

P. 56-57
The shelving unit is finished in crocodile leather. The walls, blinds and couch are in grey flannel.
The two club chairs and the pouf by Liaigre are covered with suede. Sculpture by Bernar Venet.

The office of the lady of the house, in gleaming polished sycamore.

P. 58
Chocolate-brown plastered and polished
walls in this boudoir with wall lamps by
Ralph Lauren.
The washbasin, an Esther Gutmer design in
veined marble, appears to float between its
supports, which are made of an unusual
wood with a polished finish.

P. 61-63
The sitting room beside the bedroom, with a view of the dressing room between the sliding doors. A table designed by Esther Gutmer, Ralph Lauren chairs and a Fortuny lamp.

The first floor of the main building is
devoted entirely to the owners' living space.

THE NOMADIC SPIRIT

A fter travelling through Egypt and China, the young artist Sophie Cauvin started to integrate symbols into her work that refer to eastern philosophies, particularly Taoism.

Her work radiates a meditative, timeless strength, and seeks an answer to the universal questions that surface in all civilisations. She is fascinated by eastern and primitive African art and by non-western philosophies in general.

Sophie Cauvin lives in a beautiful house designed by an architect in 1992 for his own use, although he never moved in.

The Brussels-based artist was mainly attracted by the minimalist architecture, which has a great atmosphere of calm. The property has no doors and few walls, so there is a real sense of space. Sophie Cauvin lives there with her favourite objects and pieces. The furniture is contemporary and streamlined (including designs by Christian Liaigre, Gilles de Meulemeester for Ebony and Actualine) and harmonises beautifully with the timeless eastern and African art.

Two Ethiopian village guards from the Konsô tribe welcome the visitor.

Sophie Cauvin's studio is around thirty kilometres from her home.

P. 68-69
Mercure alchimique, a mixed-technique
work by Sophie Cauvin above an Actualine
sofa. The custom-made opium table in
bamboo is by Marc Vankrinkenveld. The
standing lamp on the left is by Les Ateliers
de la Cambre.

Sophie Cauvin's work is strongly influenced by non-western civilisations.

The two club chairs at the front of the photograph are by Christian Liaigre. The daybed is by Actualine. A work by Sophie Cauvin above the antique cabinet from Michiels. To the right, a granary ladder and two statues, all from the Dogon tribe.

The beautiful lines of a pine wood: the view from Sophie Cauvin's home.

THE ULTIMATE IN SIMPLICITY

F amous couturier Edouard Vermeulen from the Natan fashion house (also see report on pages 44–51) asked architect Vincent Van Duysen to create an apartment in a building designed by Marc Corbiau, introducing an atmosphere of calm and serenity.

This large and airy apartment has an almost church-like beauty and simplicity. This is a quest for the essence of architecture and interior design. Everything is reduced to its most basic expression: simple lines, perfect symmetry, a monochrome colour palette and the strength of natural materials.

In the foreground, a padded footstool in white leather. The oak floor has a bleached finish.

An architecture that is distinguished by its monumentality and simplicity.

The bleached parquet floor extends throughout the whole apartment, further reinforcing the sense of space and harmony. The bronze dish is by John Pawson, one of the protagonists of minimalism.

P. 76-77
The bedroom, with a work of art by Stéphanie Schneider in the foreground. Lamp by Liaigre.

The bathroom also has a very simple and streamlined design, by
Vincent Van Duysen. The bath is in solid bluestone. Taps: Volevatch.

A MANOR STYLE

WITH CONTEMPORARY ACCENTS

Costermans, the construction company for exclusive homes, created this house in a French manor style on the edge of a leafy residential district with a beautiful view of the surrounding meadows.

The owner of the house aimed to create a balance between old and new, both in the finish and in the interior architecture.

Contemporary furniture was therefore selected, but with respect for the classic proportions of this villa. The project was a success: all of the authentic elements harmonise with the more streamlined furniture.

The floor in French natural stone was finished in situ. Furniture by B&B Italia and Maxalto. Lighting by Stéphane Davidts.

Costermans took inspiration from an English design to create these stairs in French oak. A wrought-iron rail with old rosace elements. Floor in Noir de Mazy stone combined with French limestone. Flamant paints.

P. 82-83
Sitting room with an antique French Louis XV fireplace. The table is by Molteni; seating by B&B Italia and Maxalto. Fabrics for curtains and blinds by Zimmer & Rohde.

P. 84-85
A sofa based on a model by Costermans and upholstered in fabrics by Luciano Marcato and Sahco Hesslein. Wall lamps by Stéphane Davidts with a Sahco Hesslein fabric. The parquet floor in French oak has an aged finish. Paints by Flamant.

The oak floor and desk (a creation by Costermans) have an aged finish. Blinds by Dedar.

Cupboard by Molteni. Curtains in Zimmer & Rohde fabrics.

The dressing room, in French oak, was designed by Costermans. Lighting by Stéphane Davidts. An oak floor in the same shade as the wardrobes.

Boudoir designed by Costermans.

NEW LIFE FOR A MANOR HOUSE

The old estate of Cothet de Lestang is part of the medieval village of Plazac, on the edge of the Périgord Noir, in the midst of a landscape of distant horizons that are dominated by the rocks that once housed the cave dwellings of earliest civilisation.

Architect Stéphane Boens has done a masterful job of restoring the local manoir of Chanloubet, a former refuge for the nobility.

This is one of those beautiful old estates that can be found in the countryside: buildings that are less spectacular than castles and which were designed for rest and relaxation.

The entrance hall with the stairs to the second floor.

P. 92-95

The interior of this manor house is focused outwards, with plenty of light coming from both the east and the west.

The stairs provide access to only two large, similar rooms on each floor.

P. 98-101
The owners' bedroom (p. 98-99) and bathroom.

A CONTEMPORARY

DESIGNER ATMOSPHERE

T his house from 1930 was built by a modernist architect who took his inspiration from Le Corbusier.

Stéphanie Laporte restored this house in collaboration with architects Jan Demeyere and Kris Carton (The Office).

The interior of the house displays a contrast between the pale shades of the floors and the furniture in dark-tinted veneer. Art is very important in this home and was selected with the advice of the Deweer Art Gallery. The look is sober, comfortable and functional: a beautiful place to live.

The kitchen block is in dark-tinted veneer with concealed handles and is finished in Emperador stone. Floor: Cotto d'Este.

A work by Andy Wauman in the hall. Floor and stairs in oak.

A chaise longue by Le Corbusier, with a work by Koen Vanmechelen.

The way through to the kitchen, with a
piece by Panamarenko on the left.

P. 106-108
The use of the same colours throughout creates an atmosphere of calm and serenity. Sitting area in shades of brown combined with paler touches.

A custom-built kitchen with an open fireplace and grill.

The parents' bathroom is connected to the dressing room and bedroom.

The office and shelving were designed by Stéphanie Laporte. Photo by Bjorn Tagemose and chairs by Bertoia. This room leads to the multifunctional space beneath the living room.

An interplay of pale and dark shades in the parents' bedroom.

A DECORATION COMPANY

IN A HISTORIC BUILDING

T rendson, the famous decoration company, is based in a distinctive historic house.

Decorators Koen Van Gestel and Suzy Clé have meticulously restored this building to create a beautiful and exclusive showroom/private interior.

This report features a number of the rooms in this unique property, all carefully designed and orchestrated by the two owners of Trendson.

The walls in the large sitting room are in silk. The medieval atmosphere and the deep armchairs create a dramatic, yet relaxed look in this impressive room with its six windows.

This mansard room is a cosy space for reading and watching TV.
The hand-printed wallpaper and the fabrics with a variety of motifs introduce a natural elegance.

The red armchair and the pile carpet lend a warm atmosphere to this snug corner of the bedroom in shades of white and black.

TABLEAU VIVANT

Olivier Dwek designed this apartment for a keen collector of contemporary art, basing the project around her impressive collection.

The large windows allow the trees to become part of the interior, forming real tableaux vivants.

All of the sliding doors disappear into the walls to create a loft atmosphere. The owner coordinated the decoration herself.

This project was created in collaboration with interior architect Coline Visse. The light and the simplicity of the space and the materials underline the strength of the works of art on display.

The large windows bring nature closer as real tableaux vivants.

Three-legged Costes chairs by Philippe Starck and art by Robert Mangold, Thomas Schütte and Moshekwa Langa. Two padded Barcelona seats by Mies Van der Rohe (at Knoll).

The central block visually separates the dining room and the sitting room, while still providing a connection between the two spaces. Left, a work by Changwa Hwang.

The suspended wall above the open fireplace can be used for video projection. Seating by Zanotta. The white piece of art on the right is by Fontana.

The master bedroom. Sliding doors with handles in brushed stainless steel allow the owners to open this space up completely or to close it off. Works by Roni Horn and Ettore Spalletti. Rocking chair by Zanotta. Lighting by Sabino.

Olivier Dwek architectural studio designed the master bathroom and Lapidis constructed it in Italian Grigio Adriatico stone. Taps by Dornbracht. Shower with built-in hammam. A custom-built dressing room in dark-tinted oak.

HOME SERIES

Volume 10 : DESIGNER HOUSES

The reports in this book are selected from the Beta-Plus collection of home-design books: www.betaplus.com
They have been compiled in a special series by Le Figaro in French language: Ma Déco

Copyright © 2009 Beta-Plus Publishing / Le Figaro
Originally published in French language

PUBLISHER
Beta-Plus Publishing
Termuninck 3
B – 7850 Enghien
Belgium
www.betaplus.com
info@betaplus.com

PHOTOGRAPHY
Jo Pauwels

DESIGN
Polydem - Nathalie Binart

TRANSLATIONS
Laura Watkinson

ISBN : 9789089440419

Printed in China

P. 124-125
The dining room in a former sculptor's studio, furnished by
Christine Lemaître and Amélie de Borchgrave d'Altena.

P. 126-127
Interior architect Jean-Marc Vynckier transformed this
eighteenth-century hunting lodge to create a modern home.